T0128126

Other works contributed to by Enoch Elijah:

Creation of the Glorious Church
What Must Come to Pass
Insights for Believers

God Is!

The Ultimate Reality

Enoch Elijah

WESTBOW
PRESS®
A DIVISION OF THOMAS NELSON
& ZONDERVAN

WestBow Press books may be ordered through booksellers or by contacting:

WestBow Press
A Division of Thomas Nelson & Zondervan
1663 Liberty Drive
Bloomington, IN 47403
www.westbowpress.com
1 (866) 928-1240

Scripture taken from the King James Version of the Bible.

ISBN: 978-1-9736-9788-6 (sc)
ISBN: 978-1-9736-9789-3 (hc)
ISBN: 978-1-9736-9787-9 (e)

Library of Congress Control Number: 2020913015

Print information available on the last page.

WestBow Press rev. date: 08/04/2020

Dedication

This book is written and dedicated to everyone who has ever asked the question, "is God real" or has questions about what His existence means for them?

Throughout history the desire for answers about the Lord has caused many to discover what God has to offer.

God is the ultimate reality, supreme, final and the fundamental power in all reality.

> *That the God of our Lord Jesus Christ, the Father of glory, may give unto you the spirit of wisdom and revelation in the knowledge of him:*
>
> *The eyes of your understanding being enlightened; that ye may know (comprehend) what is the hope of his calling, and what the riches of the glory of his inheritance in the saints,*
>
> *And what is the exceeding greatness of his power to us-ward who believe, according to the working of his mighty power,*
>
> *(Ephesians 1:17-19)*

Epigraph

The key to the revelation of the existence and supremacy of God is linked to our beliefs. Do you have faith that He is, and that Jesus Christ is the mediator between us and Him, mending our broken relationship?

> *But without faith it is impossible to please him: for he, that cometh to God must <u>believe</u> that he is, and that he is a rewarder of them that diligently seek him.*
>
> *(Hebrews 11:6)*

Contents

Contents

Preface

In November of 2019, my third book "Insights for Believers" was published. In December, the Lord begin to deal with me about Him being a reality, "God Is".

Now I realize three months later with the outbreak of a virus we must believe and know that He is and that He is in control.

When I was 11 or 12 years old; I had been to church. Had seen and heard my grandmother operate in the Spirit. Yet, that did not create the belief within me that God existed, and that He is a rewarder of those who seek Him.

One day I was laying in the front yard in the grass, watching the clouds and I asked myself is there truly a God?

I then heard a response within me, "you shall see me in my glory!" I thank Him for choosing me from the foundation of the world. He knew each of us before we were born.

Nine years passed before I accepted Christ; yet during the nine years I knew that He existed even though I did not serve Him.

The key to the revelation that "God Is", is hidden in the intuition within each of us.

"Intuition is the ability to understand something immediately, without the need for conscious reasoning."

What is your perception and understanding of God or lack thereof?

This book will raise questions and give biblical *truths* to provide answers to how the Lord shaped and developed the history of the creation to fully help us assess His plan to convert us into His most cherished assets as we develop the knowledge and understanding of who He is.

> He that dwelleth in the secret place of the most High shall abide under the shadow of the Almighty.
>
> I will say of the Lord, He is my refuge and my fortress: my God; in him will I trust.
>
> (Psalms 91:1-2)

Introduction

GOD IS!

"Be" is the first and third person of the word "is". The word "be" means to exist. Therefore, God exists!

God is incorporeal having no material existence, no body or form.

He is omniscient (all knowing), omnipotent (all powerful), and omnipresent (in all places at once).

> *God is a Spirit: and they that worship him must*
> *worship him in spirit and in truth.*
>
> *(John 4:24)*

Jesus said:

> *All things are delivered to me of my Father: and*
> *no man knoweth who the Son is, but the Father;*
> *and who the Father is, but the Son, and he to*
> *whom the Son will reveal him.*
>
> *(Luke 10:22)*

To know God, you must first know the Son; and the Son (Jesus) will reveal Him to you by the Holy Spirit.

The Lord illustrates His existence through the biblical truths of Him being the author and finisher of the world that is and is to come.

> *I am Alpha and Omega, the beginning, and the ending, saith the Lord, which is, and which was, and which is to come, the Almighty.*
>
> *(Revelation 1:8)*

He accomplishes His introduction by revealing His sovereignty in the acts He orchestrated during the creation of the earth and His guiding hand over the events in history. He shows us He is sovereign and all powerful.

Yet unless we are enlightened through Jesus by the Holy Spirit revealing the Father to us, we cannot comprehend who God is; even though creation is the reality of His existence. A picture of His creative power.

God reveals Himself through interaction (communication) and interrelationship (how He relates to us). He told Moses to tell the children of Israel, the God of your fathers had sent him; Moses asked, "what if they ask what his name is (Exodus 3:13)." He told Moses to answer them I AM that I AM; tell them I AM sent you (Exodus 3:14). This is an example of God's interaction (communication).

In Exodus 6:3 the Lord told Moses that Abraham, Isaac, and Jacob knew Him as God Almighty[1]. El Shaddai is the Hebrew word for God Almighty; it means the full riches of God's grace and mercy. That He is willing to pour out every good and perfect gift.

Abraham traveled from place to place obtaining wealth as he worked through life events (dreams, fears, and battles: Genesis chapter 12 through chapter 22) dealing with Sarai, Lot, Hagar, Ishmael, the birth and offering of Isaac. The Lord blessed and multiplied Abraham (Genesis 22:17). The Lord was truly El Shaddai to him.

This is how God showed interrelationship through the events of Abraham's life revealing He was a giver of grace, mercy, and every good gift?

Jacob's[2] name in Hebrew means supplanted (Genesis 27:36), meaning to replace. The story of him and his mother's trickery can be found in Genesis 27:15-30.

Jacob tricked his father to believe he was Esau so he could get the blessing as the oldest son. Yet, the Lord blessed him in his dealing with Laban, his mother's brother (Genesis 27:43 – 30:27). This is a sure example of God showing His grace, mercy, and pouring out good and perfect gifts.

God said, "they knew me as God Almighty (El Shaddai) but they did not know me as Jehovah."

Jehovah[3] means self-existent and eternal. God is eternal! In Exodus 6:6 the Lord God tells Moses, "tell the children of Israel I Am the Lord." The word Lord here is the same word as Jehovah in verse three.

Just as today we must move from knowing God as a giver of grace and mercy; the one who gives every perfect gift to knowing the God that is self-existent and eternal with the capability to fulfill miraculous purpose in our lives.

The focus of this work is to illustrate that God is more than a giver of gifts. Grace and mercy are important; they are the catalyst for salvation; in this hour as in the hour of Israel's deliverance from Egypt, we must know Him as a self-existent, eternal, and limit-less; to fully enjoy the life He has given us now and in the future.

> *And because ye are sons, God hath sent forth the*
> *Spirit of his Son into your hearts, crying, Abba*
> *Father.*
>
> *(Galatians 4:6)*

The word Abba[4] signifies trust without reasoning as a child has for their father.

God's purpose is for us to know Him as our father and the author of our future. The Lord *which is, and which was, and which is to come;* to be like Him (through Christ) is to truly know Him.

The phrase, *which is, and which was, and which is to come* is a statement that illustrates eternity. We are eternal beings. You are alive now (which is), and Jeremiah 1:5 states God knew us before we were formed in our mothers belly (which was), and John 3:15 says, "if we believe on Jesus Christ we shall have everlasting life (is to come).

Therefore, ask the Lord now to give you a new perspective of who He is and who you are.

*Because the creature itself also shall be delivered
from the bondage of corruption into the glorious
liberty of the children of God.*

*For we know that the whole creation groaneth
and travaileth in pain together until now.*

*And not only they, but ourselves also, which
have the first fruits of the Spirit, even we ourselves
groan within ourselves, waiting for the adoption,
to wit, the redemption of our body.*

*For we are saved by hope: but hope that is
seen is not hope: for what a man seeth, why doth
he yet hope for?*

*But if we hope for that we see not, then do we
with patience wait for it.*

(Romans 8:21-25)

The word creature[5] in this verse references the creative act
within itself. The act of creation had the over-riding purpose to
provide an avenue for mankind to be regenerated and delivered
from bondage.

t r u t h

Creation Rationale

Rationale is a set of reasons or intention for a set
of thoughts or actions.

(American Dictionary)

In this "Truth" I will discuss my thoughts on the reason and
intention for creation and how it is linked to the plan of God.

This is the first truth because it rejects the concept that
God created the heavens and earth as a second thought after
Lucifer's fall.

God uses the stories of the bible to create pictures that reveal
hidden meanings. Genesis 1:26 details the creation of human
life. Human life without the influence of the Holy Spirit.

I know this because Genesis 2:7 describes spiritual life after
God breath into Adam creating in him a living soul. The breath
exhaled into Adam caused eternal life by the power of the Holy
Spirit.

Why were the heavens and the earth created? They were
established by the inspiration of the Lord God for the purpose

of developing a family of worshipers out of the struggles and influences of independence and unrighteousness. Life's journey helps us know how sin can impact our lives. Without the fall of Lucifer and the other angels, there would never have been a need for the perfecting process that was established to ensure an eternity without a future possibility of unrighteousness.

Spiritual beings are capable of thoughts related to self-gratification which can lead to actions outside the will of the Lord God. This was demonstrated by Lucifer's revolt in the spirit realm impacting the relationship that was established between God and him.

Hebrews 4:10 shows that when we enter the rest of God, we ceased from our own works as God did in Genesis chapter two before he created Adam. Revelations 7:9-14 is a picture of God giving His people rest from the tribulation of the world.

I believe from Genesis to Revelations the plan for man's salvation was the overriding principle from the beginning until the end.

> *Thou art the anointed cherub the covereth; and I have set thee so: thou wast upon the holy mountain of God; thou hast walked up and down the midst of the stones of fire.*
>
> *Thou wast perfect in thy ways from the day that thou wast created, till iniquity was found in thee.*
>
> *(Ezekiel 28:14-15)*

Lucifer was the covering, the defense[6], and the hedge of protection of where the spirit of God dwelt. He was created for this purpose. This is signified in the above scripture where fire[7] illustrates God's presence and the stones[8] illustrates the construction of the holy mountain[9] of God. Ezekiel chapter 28 gives the indication that Lucifer was a covering for the essence of God.

In Luke 10:18 Jesus said, "I beheld Satan as lightning fall from heaven." Satan fell from the presence of God after he was cast out of his position as the anointed cherub[10] due to iniquity within him.

When God gave instruction to build the tabernacle in Exodus chapter 25; He was giving the illustration of the reality of something very real in heaven.

> *And thou shalt make two cherubims of gold, of beaten work shalt thou make them, in the two ends of the mercy seat.*
>
> *And make one cherub on the one end, and the other cherub on the other end: even of the mercy seat shall ye make the cherubims on the two ends thereof.*
>
> *And the cherubims shall stretch forth their wings on high, covering the mercy seat with their wings, and their faces shall look one to another; toward the mercy seat shall the faces of the cherubims be.*
>
> *(Exodus 25:18-20)*

Exodus chapter 25 starts the discussion of the tabernacle worship and the offering of sacrifice for sin. A picture of what Christ did at the cross. A structure that was established in heaven that shows the pattern established to provide mercy to mankind through Christ's sacrifice before there was a creation.

> *And I will put enmity between thee and the woman, and between thy seed and her seed; it shall bruise thy head, and thou shalt bruise his heel.*
>
> *(Genesis 3:15)*

God had the plan already in place for salvation. In the above scripture the Lord informs the serpent that Christ would be born, and He would bruise his head.

"God Is"; only He could set a plan in place and execute it thousands of years later.

Was the timing of Lucifer's fall prior to creation, simultaneous to creation or after creation?

> *He that committeth sin is of the devil; for the devil sinneth from the beginning. For this purpose, the Son of God was manifested, that he might destroy the works of the devil.*
>
> *(1 John 3:8)*

Creation itself is now and was then the process for God to develop spiritual beings that would serve Him because they want to; there by destroying the work of the devil. Remember angels were created to worship God and Lucifer's iniquity influenced that original structure.

I believe Lucifer's fall was early into the overall creation process as the above verse states. Remember God is eternal, Psalms 90:4 says, "a thousand years in thy sight are but as yesterday when it is past"; so the span of time between Lucifer's fall and his visit to the garden could have been thousands of years. Time is relative in eternity! This battle between light and darkness has been played out since the beginning until now.

The resentment of Adam who was created in God's image with a free will and cherished of God, led Lucifer to want to destroy the relationship. He showed up in the garden persuaded Eve to have thoughts outside the instruction God gave; the same as he desired of being exalted beyond his created position.

Even though Lucifer can travel back and forth from the earth into the presence of God accusing mankind as seen in Revelation 12:10; telling God we aren't worthy of His mercy because the fact is he (Lucifer) is the unworthy one that created the need for salvation and influenced our separation from God. Remember I mentioned in the introduction that the word creature in Romans 8:21 meant the creative act within itself. Meaning mankind as a part of the creation process would be recreated in the image of God through this environment where spiritual beings could work out their feelings of self-gratification which would allow them to conform to the will of God and be suitable for eternity. An eternity where bondage and corruption would not exist.

> *Thou hast been in Eden the garden of God; every*
> *precious stone was thy covering, the sardius,*
> *topaz, and the diamond, the beryl, the onyx,*
> *and the jasper, the sapphire, the emerald, and*
> *the carbuncle, and gold: the workmanship of thy*
> *tabrets and of thy pipes was prepared in thee in*
> *the day thou wast created.*
>
> *(Ezekiel 28:13)*

Ezekiel 28:13 illustrates him as an instrument of worship. The word tabrets[11] means tambourine an instrument used to make music for worship.

This verse links the events in the garden with Adam and Eve back to Lucifer. Was his fall from his former position with God before the events in the garden or did the events in the garden cause his fall? I believe Lucifer had already fallen before he interacted with Eve.

The events in the garden was a calculated effort to take over God's creation which Adam had authority to rule. Which means Lucifer wanted to rule over what God had created.

> *The sons of God saw the daughters of men that*
> *they were fair; and they took them wives of all*
> *which they chose.*
>
> *(Genesis 6:2)*

Verses three through seven give us insight to the offspring of humans and angels.

Because of the activities of these fallen angels (followers of Lucifer) and the minds of men being on evil continually is the reason God had to destroy mankind with the flood.

Lucifer has already been removed from his position as the cherish cherub. He and the angels that followed him are still spiritual entities and Lucifer can still go before the throne of God (Job 1:6 and Revelation 12:10) but his ability is diminished because of the sacrifice of Jesus Christ.

> *By the multitude of thy merchandise they have*
> *filled the midst of thee with violence, and thou*
> *hast sinned: therefore I will cast thee as profane*
> *out of the mountain of God: and I will destroy*
> *thee, O covering cherub, from the midst of the*
> *stones of fire.*
>
> *Thine heart was lifted because of thy beauty,*
> *thou hast corrupted thy wisdom by reason of thy*
> *brightness: I will cast thee to the ground, I will*
> *lay thee before kings, that they may behold thee.*
> *(Ezekiel 28:16-17)*

What was Lucifer's iniquity? He wanted recognition and to be exalted above God by reason of his beauty which caused him to be cast out of the presence of God. Then he wanted to control creation due to his resentment of the relationship God had with Adam and Eve; which caused the judgement of God to establish a future event by executing the sentence for Lucifer to be cased to the ground in judgement.

*And there was war in heaven: Michael and his
angels fought against the dragon; and the dragon
fought and his angels,*

*And prevailed not; neither was their place
found any more in heaven.*

*And the great dragon was cast out, that
old serpent, called the devil, and satan, which
deceiveth the whole world: he was cast out into
the earth, and his angels were cast out with him.*

(Revelation 12:7-9)

The creation is the battle ground between Lucifer and the
Lord.

*And when the dragon saw that he was cast
unto the earth, he persecuted the woman which
brought forth the man child.*

(Revelation 12:13)

This verse informs us in the future when the devil is cast to
the ground, he will take his judgement out on the Israeli people,
the earthly family of Jesus. Just as stated in Genesis 3:15. At
this time satan will continue his revengeful actions against the
children of Israel.

Once again, the rationale for creations is a basis for a course
of action to deal with the possibility of spiritual beings having
independent desires which could lead to actions outside the will
of the Lord God. We are now on the journey to return to the
family of God to give Him glory.

God would not be omniscient (all knowing) if creation was an after-thought, the result of the fall of Lucifer.

His vision was to have a kingdom which He established with beings that served Him and displayed His attributes. We are traveling through a land to get to a land (New Jerusalem) that was destined for us before there was time (Revelation 21:1-2).

"God Is!"

The reality of creation is that it was God's plan from the start to account for Lucifer's fall and the orchestration of the heavens and earth to be the proving ground for man to overcome Lucifer and Adam's failures by receiving salvation and eternity through Christ.

His goal is to work through the spirit to cause the inner man to realize who he is in Christ and have the knowledge that God has through Christ.

Did you ever think you could have the knowledge that God has?

truth

Understanding

The attributes of God are linked to His wisdom and understanding of all things.

> *Counsel is mine, and sound wisdom: I am understanding; I have strength.*
>
> *(Proverbs 8:14)*

> *The Lord possessed me in the beginning of his way, before his works of old.*
>
> *I was set up from everlasting, from the beginning, or ever the earth was.*
>
> *When there were no depths, I was brought forth; when there were not fountains abounding with water.*
>
> *Before the mountains were settled, before the hills was I brought forth:*

> *While as yet he had not made the earth, nor the fields, nor the highest part of the dust of the world.*
>
> *When he prepared the heavens, I was there: when he set a compass upon the face of the depth:*
>
> *When he established the clouds above: when he strengthened the fountains of the deep:*
>
> *When he gave to the sea his decree, that the waters should not pass his commandment: when he appointed the foundations of the earth:*
>
> *Then I was by him, as one brought up with him: and I was daily his delight, rejoicing always before him;*
>
> *(Proverbs 8:22-30)*

Proverbs 8:14 communicates two important aspects of God, wisdom and understanding. Both words have the inference of being interconnected with the personality of God.

As God began the work of creation, He had the ability to understand from the depths of His infinite wisdom[12] to substantiate and support His creative work. Understanding[13] in verse 14 is defined as the act of understanding. This means vision, intelligence, knowledge, imagination, and consideration caused God to proceed and act on His thoughts of creation through His capability. Understanding is speaking in first person when it says, "the Lord possessed[14] me" in verse 22, which means to own and possess the capability to create the idea and possess the ability to establish creation and its purpose. This word (possessed) is strongly linked to the vision God had.

Its definition illustrates the possession of understanding was before creation began. Allowing the Lord to frame creation from the beginning for the purpose of reconciling man back to Him. He understood and foresaw His creative work; no, He envisioned the creation before it was created.

Simply put understanding represents every capability that God possess. It is twofold first it was the knowledge to create heaven, earth, and the many life forms; second it had depth of intuition into the changing elements of life for its duration spanning the existence of mankind.

Life in Adams day was much different than life today. God's depth of intuition of the progress of man's intellect and knowledge illustrates His omniscient (knowing all through all of eternity).

An architect designs blueprints for a house. He envisions the amenities of the house before he draws the plans. This is what the Lord has done.

> *Thus saith God the Lord, he that created the heavens, and stretched them out; he that spread forth the earth, and that which cometh out of it; he that giveth breath unto the people upon it, and spirit to them that walk therein:*
>
> *I the Lord have called thee in righteousness, and will hold thine hand, and will keep thee, and*

> *give thee for a covenant of the people, for a light*
> *of the Gentiles;*
>
> *To open the blind eyes, to bring out the*
> *prisoners from the prison, and them that sit in*
> *darkness out of the prison house.*
>
> *I am the Lord: that is my name: and my glory*
> *will I not give to another, neither my praise to*
> *graven images.*
>
> *Behold, the former things are come to pass,*
> *and new things do I declare: before they spring*
> *forth I tell you of them.*
>
> *(Isaiah 42:5-9)*

Jesus Christ has made a way for us to receive righteousness, a covenant with the Lord, deliverance, and light to gain the understanding of God. The understanding that allows God to communicate the new things He is doing before they happen.

As we give reverence to God, we will begin to gain insight into the special ability of the Lord to fashion whatever He will; as we begin to know how sacred He is; then we can understand His acts.

> *Thou art worthy, O Lord, to receive glory and*
> *honour and power: for thou hast created all*
> *things, and for thy pleasure they are and were*
> *created.*
>
> *(Revelation 4:11)*

Words like intelligence, knowledge or consideration cannot begin to describe the intellectual power of God. We see God's personality (intellectual and moral character) through the intuitive process of how He structured creation.

> Intuitiveness is knowing something without rational thought or learning; it is instinctive.
>
> (Dictionary.com)

Therefore, I believe God's intuition is instinctive, which is the essence of why He is omniscient (all knowing).

So, the thought and knowledge to bring about creation was within God before the earth was formed; from everlasting as Proverbs 8:23 states.

> *The fear of the LORD is the beginning of wisdom: and the knowledge of the holy is understanding.*
>
> *(Proverbs 9:10)*

> *Wisdom is the principal thing; therefore, get wisdom: and with all thy getting get understanding.*
>
> *(Proverbs 4:7)*

We must gain experience with God to gain understanding. The knowledge of Christ helps us to begin the act of bridging the gulf from the natural to the spiritual.

> *"For whatsoever is born of God overcometh the*
> *world: and this is the victory that overcometh the*
> *world, even our faith;*
> *Who is he that overcometh the world, but he*
> *that believeth that Jesus is the Son of God."*
>
> *(1 John 5:4-5)*

The Greek word for overcometh[15] means to subdue, overcome, conquer, prevail, or get victory. For us to understand who "God Is" we must first conquer the worldly thought process.

Once we accept Christ, we are filled with the knowledge of His will in all wisdom and spiritual understand through the study of the Word.

> *That their hearts might be comforted, being*
> *knit together in love, and unto all riches of*
> *the full assurance of understanding, to the*
> *acknowledgement of the mystery of God, and of*
> *the Father, and of Christ;*
> *In whom are hid all the treasures of wisdom*
> *and knowledge.*
>
> *(Colossians 2:2-3)*

The word understanding[16] in this verse is to mentally put knowledge and understanding together through your intellect. This act of linking what you have learned of Christ allowing the Spirit of God to teach you the mysteries[17] of God.

This mystery is outside the range of assisted natural apprehension, it can only be made known by divine revelation by the Spirit of God.

God's goal is for us to know Him. Do you know He is real, the orchestrator not only of the plans of the earth but also the plans for your life? Have you sensed His presence at different times in your life?

Genesis 3:15 is a prophecy of eternal life through Christ; please realize Adam and Eve were eternal until the fall (Genesis 3:22-23). If they were not, why did God drive them out of Eden and a flaming sword turning every way was placed to keep the way of the tree of life (Genesis 3:24) to prevent them from eating thereof and living forever. The knowledge of good and evil would have to be dealt with to prevent evil from existing throughout eternity.

This sword is the Word of God!

Let us look at Cain and Abel.

> *And Adam knew Eve his wife, and she conceived, and bare Cain, and said, I have gotten a man from the Lord.*
>
> *And she again bare his brother Abel. And Abel was a keeper of sheep, but Cain was a tiller of the ground.*
>
> *And in the process of time it came to pass, that Cain brought of the fruit of the ground an offering unto the Lord.*

> *And Abel, he also brought of the firstlings of his flock and of the fat thereof. And the Lord had respect unto Abel and to his offering:*
>
> *But unto Cain and to his offering he had not respect. And Cain was very wroth, and his countenance fell.*
>
> *(Genesis 4:1-5)*

Abel made a blood sacrifice. This shows they understood the requirement of blood as an offering for remission of separation from God.

This is an excellent picture of Christ's sacrifice for remission of our sin.

> *And Cain talked with Abel his brother: and it came to pass, when they were in the field, that Cain rose up against Abel his brother, and slew him.*
>
> *(Genesis 4:8)*

> *And Cain went out from the presence of the Lord, and dwelt in the land of Nod, on the east of Eden.*
>
> *(Genesis 4:16)*

Cain kills Abel out of jealousy and rebellion. Not wanting to do things God's way. Just as Lucifer was jealous of Adam and put a plan in place to cause Adam to lose his eternal place in God resulting in death (Genesis 3:22-24).

Cain was now no longer in the presence of God becoming a vagrant wandering around in the land of Nod.[18] This is a picture of us before we come into the knowledge of accepting the sacrifice of Christ.

To possess understanding is to realize that God intuitively had the knowledge and capability to bring the vision of the heavens, the earth, and mankind's future to pass.

t r u t h

Resolution for Darkness

"Resolution is the action of solving a problem or dispute."

God's purpose was to resolve and eliminate the possibility of darkness in His kingdom forever.

God uses simplistic language to describe complex concepts such as light and darkness to illustrate the concepts of right and wrong; good and evil; righteousness and unrighteousness. The phrase light or darkness requires no further illustration; He set the identifier of light as equivalent to good and righteousness; and darkness as equivalent to evil and unrighteousness.

Being human we require observation and must process what we see or hear to determine if an action is good or evil; righteous or unrighteous; these require the assessment of emotions, thoughts, and actions we observe to help us define and distinguish the difference.

In Truth 1 I mentioned the fall of Lucifer was at the earliest part of creation. God knew there was a possibility of sin (darkness) in the heavenlies and in the earth He would create.

> *In the beginning God created the heaven and the earth.*
>
> *And the earth was without form, and void; and darkness was upon the face of the deep. And the Spirit of God moved upon the face of the waters.*
>
> *And God said, Let there be light: and there was light.*
>
> *And God saw the light, that it was good: and God divided the light from the darkness.*
>
> *And God called the light Day, and the darkness he called Night. And the evening and the morning were the first day.*
>
> *(Genesis 1:1-5)*

When God said let there be light in verse three and divided the light from the darkness that was not the development of a 24-hour day. In verse five it simply says he called light - day and darkness – night; the evening and the morning were the first day.

Remember day, night, and establishment of time and seasons as we know it was not created until Genesis 1:14-19 on day four of creation.

> In verses two and four the word darkness is figurative of ignorance, death, misery, and destruction. The word light in verses three and four references luminaries in every sense such as light, happiness, and inspiration.
>
> (Strong's Expanded Exhaustive Concordance)

The word day[19] in verse five is more of a reference to a period or a moment in time as a reference when something happened. Remember time as we know it has not been established yet, God is communicating this description during a period in the realm of eternity.

The words light and darkness[20] alludes to a broader message based on their meaning. Ignorance – death - destruction are words that are more linked to a spiritual condition and allows us to go back to the root cause of man being without God, not the establishment of the period when its dark outside. Light - happiness - inspiration is more linked to emotion and the fact we can see the result of righteousness as light[21].

Therefore Genesis 1:1-5 is documenting the physical attributes that made the earth without form and void covered with darkness. A confused empty space, a vast plane of nothingness without order.

Humans are made up of stardust. We have 97% of the same type of atoms as the stars in the galaxy. Elements like oxygen and carbon are at the galaxy's center. We were created supernatural. This points to a universal creator.

Light is illumination, another term for illuminance is physics.

> Physics is the branch of science concerned with the nature and properties of matter and energy; the physical properties and phenomena that creates something.
>
> (Merriam-Webster)

The Lord established the scientific concepts that made it possible for the earth to be formed and for ground (the earth) to be established. Yet, there is even more than the natural purpose at work here. There is also a spiritual purpose.

God divided the light from the darkness, He distinguished their difference (verse four). This is a metaphor. A metaphor is when we refer to something by mentioning something else. Light and darkness are metaphors for the difference between what God is and what Lucifer became after his rebellion.

God is mentioning light and darkness; day and night but I believe he is insinuating a spiritual state that He would rectify through the events of creation and Jesus Christ.

> *We have also a more sure word of prophecy;*
> *whereunto ye do well that ye take heed, as unto*
> *a light that shineth in a dark place, until the day*
> *dawn, and the day star arise in your hearts:*
> *(2 Peter 1:19)*

Peter is clarifying what happened in Genesis 1:1-5. The dawning of the day in your heart will bring light in the dark places within you. This is not necessarily only speaking of the sin nature; this is also referencing the capability to comprehend with in us the plans of God.

John also used the same metaphor of light and darkness to illustrate deliverance from sin due to the influence of Lucifer.

In him was life; and the life was the light of men.
And the light shineth in darkness; and the
darkness comprehended it not.

(John 1:4-5)

The light that John was talking about was life[22] as God has it, which He had within Himself. The light[23] that was given can be seen and as reaching the mind revealing Christ. This light drove out darkness[24] that had blinded us. The darkness could not comprehend[25] how we can be delivered from sin simply by laying hold of the truth possessing it as our own.

Let us see how John 1:1-5 and Genesis 1:1-5 are mirror images of each other. They both give dialog describing creation.

They both mentioned that *God spoke* (Genesis: God said; John: The Word was with God and the Word was God; all things were created by God's words).

They both *mention light and darkness* (Genesis: that God divided light and darkness; John: light shined in darkness and darkness comprehend it not).

They both detail the *presence of the Holy Spirit* (Genesis: The Spirit of God moved on the face of the waters; John: in him was life through the Spirit).

God created the opportunity for eternity in the first five verses of Genesis. Notice the phrase, "God said." The entity that was doing the talking was Jesus (the Word of God) speaking our world into existence.

It is the Holy Ghost that enables us to be filled with life (Genesis 2:7 and God formed Adam and breathed the breath of life (His Spirit) into his nostrils; Acts 2:2-4 a rush and mighty wind filled the house and they were all filled with the Holy Ghost).

The Spirit[26] hovered over the face of the waters when the earth was dark and without form a vast nothingness (Genesis 1:2). The word Spirit in this verse has the meaning of wind by resemblance of breath; a violent exhalation; figuratively life.

I am amazed how the Lord used His identity (who He is: father, word, and spirit) to orchestrates creation and the course of everlasting life through those same realities. From the start He provided clues that it was all about the plan of salvation; deliverance from the desires implanted by Lucifer.

> *The earth is the Lord's and the fulness thereof; the world, and they that dwell therein.*
>
> *For he hath founded it upon the seas (waters) and established it upon the floods.*
>
> *Who shall ascend into the hill of the Lord? Or who shall stand in his holy place?*
>
> *He that hath clean hands, and a pure heart; who hath not lifted up his soul unto vanity, nor sworn deceitfully.*
>
> *He shall receive the blessing from the Lord, and righteousness from the God of his salvation.*
>
> *(Psalms 24:1-5)*

If you can resist vanity and *be filled* with God's spirit you will demonstrate the attributes that are pleasing to the Lord;

God will bless you and provide righteousness through the sacrifice of Christ.

> *But ye are a chosen generation, a royal priesthood,*
> *a holy nation, a peculiar people; that ye should*
> *shew forth the praises of him who hath called you*
> *out of darkness into his marvelous light:*
>
> *(1 Peter 2:9)*

The spirit of God expelled darkness. We must discover how the Godhead renews and regenerates us. Which allows us to walk in the new life God intended for us.

Have you sought to be filled with His spirit?

truth

Father, Son, Holy Spirit

The essence of God is the sum of the Father, the Son, and the Holy Spirt; these three beings are intrinsic to Him. They are the illustrations provided to show the natural man His personality and how He interacts with us to move us from the natural to the spiritual. Yet He is more than the sum of the three.

THE FATHER

> *And God said, Let us make man in our image, after our likeness: and let them have dominion over the fish of the sea, and over the fowl of the air, and over the cattle, and over all earth, and over every creeping thing that creepth upon the earth.*
>
> *(Genesis 1:26)*

God rules over the universe and mankind was to rule over creation.

The word God[27] in this verse is the Hebrew word El-o-heem. The word is plural signifying more than one. This speaks to the relationship of the three persons of the Godhead: Father, Son, and Holy Spirit.

We are in God's image[28], a resemblance and a representative figure of God. Our pattern[29] (likeness) is based on the specifications from which God made in accordance with His characteristics having dominion; specifications were based on the triune structure of God. The structure of mankind is mind (reasoning capability), soul (what puts thoughts into action), and spirit (what makes us eternal). This is the sum of mankind, just as the Father, the Son, and the Holy Spirit is the sum of God. Our make up (mind, soul, spirit) is in direct correlation to the Father, Son and Spirt.

> *For the word of God is quick, and powerful, and sharper than any twoedged sword, piercing even to the dividing asunder of soul and spirit, and of the joints and marrow, and is a discerner of the thoughts and intents of the heart.*
>
> *Neither is there any creature that is not manifest in his sight: but all things are naked and opened unto the eyes of him with whom we have to do.*
>
> *(Hebrews 4:12-13)*

To understand the depths of God we must gain insights as to how His spirit interacts with ours. Our finiteness must understand the infinite. And, that can only be shared by the spirit of God with our internal man (the dividing asunder of soul and spirit). The spirit of God can communicate with our spirit by working through the inner man.

Our soul is the part of us which is influenced by our mind (what we have learned naturally), will, and emotion. Therefore, the natural man cannot obtain the knowledge that God has because he does not operate in the spirit.

> *But the natural man receiveth not the things of the Spirit of God: for they are foolishness unto him: neither can he know them, because they are spiritually discerned.*
>
> *(1 Corinthians 2:14)*

Our desires and decisions are mainly influenced by the mind, will, and emotion.

Hebrews 4:12 mentions the word of God is quick and powerful sharper than a two-edged sword. This is how the spirit deals with our inner man, helping us align with the Father.

The Bibles intent is to help us make the connection of the intent of God. If we understand His intent, we will understand Him and His purpose.

The triune nature of God the Father helps us to understand our own makeup of being formed in God's image as spiritual beings. It represents how He intended for us to be like Him.

THE WORD IS THE SON *(Jesus Christ)*

> *That which was from the beginning, which we have heard, which we have seen with our eyes, which we have looked upon, and our hands have handled, of the Word of life;*
>
> *(For the life was manifested, and we have seen it, and bear witness, and shew unto you that eternal life, which was with the Father, and was manifested unto us;)*
>
> *That which we have seen and heard declare we unto you, that ye also may have fellowship with us; and truly our fellowship is with the Father, and with his Son Jesus Christ.*
>
> *And these things write we unto you, that your joy may be full.*
>
> *This is the message which we have heard of him, and declare unto you, that God is light, and in him is no darkness at all.*
>
> *(1 John 1:1-5)*

God loved the world so much, that He gave His only begotten Son. Whosoever believeth in Him will have everlasting life.

Our challenge is to receive the light provided and gain understanding of God's place in our lives.

Jesus is what created everything, so the creator of the world sacrificed Himself for creation, setting it free from the control of Lucifer.

THE SPIRIT

God is Spirit: and they that worship him must worship him in spirit and in truth.

(John 4:24)

God is Spirit! He cannot be seen with the naked eye, He cannot be touched by our hands, He cannot be the substance of our imagination because He beyond our thoughts. But he does feel our infirmity as he speaks to us through the Holy Ghost. Listen to the spirit and be made whole.

One thing have I desired of the Lord, that will I seek after; that I may dwell in the house of the Lord all the days of my life, to behold the beauty of the Lord, and to enquire in his temple.

For in the time of trouble he shall hide me in his pavilion: in the secret of his tabernacle shall he hide me; he shall set me up upon a rock.

And now shall mine head be lifted up above mine enemies round about me: therefore will I offer in his tabernacle sacrifices of joy; I will sing, yea, I will sing praises unto the Lord.

Hear, O Lord, when I cry with my voice: have mercy also upon me, and answer me.

When thou saidst, Seek ye my face; my heart said unto thee, Thy face, Lord, will I seek.

(Psalms 27:4-8)

This passage helps us to know it is about worship of the Lord from a pure heart that desires truth, while seeking the fulness of His presence in your life. There is no other way! Then the Holy Ghost can unstop our ears and open our eyes.

THE GODHEAD WORKS IN UNISON

> *For there are three that bear record in heaven, the Father, the Word, and the Holy Ghost: and these three are one.*
>
> *And there are three that bear witness in earth, the spirit, and the water, and the blood: and these three agree in one.*
>
> *(1 John 5:7-8)*

The *Holy Ghost* documents the record in heaven and the Spirit bears witness in the earth of the documented plan and acts of God through us and the self-willed acts we perform. Notice there are two independent functions of the Spirit of God. The Holy Ghost bearing record in heaven of the established truth and the Spirit bearing witness of the record from heaven in the earth.

The *Holy Ghost* is referenced in heaven and bears record: a record affirms what has been experienced and documented; like a court reporter in a trial.

The Holy Ghost in Heaven supports the validity of the record recorded in Heaven of God's initial purpose of mankind and His creation. This is the distinction of what we will witness as we come to the realization that "God Is" and the Lord God will perform through us. Having the full power of the Godhead behind and within us.

We must begin to see ourselves through the lens of the Lord through what the Holy Ghost has affirmed for us from heaven. Not on what is seen or understood in the realm of the earth. Know that your capability in God is abundantly more than you have ever imaged. Begin to realize your progression from faith to faith and glory to glory.

> *But when you pray, use not vain repetitions, as the heathen do; for they think that they shall be heard for their much speaking.*
> *Be not ye therefore like unto them; for your Father knoweth what things ye have need of, before ye ask Him.*
>
> *(Matthew 6:7-8)*

Do you believe it is possible from the start of time for God to know everything you would need and ask thousands of years in the future?

The possibility of answer to prayers being known by God before we ask is a fact. The answer is established in heaven before you ask. Even sometimes when we hope for a different answer.

As a child I would get up early on Saturday morning to see replays of a college football team in Louisiana.

In those days cable TV was just beginning to become an industry. I watched TV with an antenna. If I adjusted the antenna exactly right, I could get the replays of the games.

I remember thinking it would be great when I was older if I could live in Louisiana. As I served the Lord, He did direct my path to Louisiana.

A year after I stopped traveling with my work the Lord brought to my remembrance all the places I had hoped as a child to visit; He enabled it to happen. Glory to His Name!

Yes, He gives you the desires of your heart as you serve Him! Taking consideration of your thoughts and wishes; just as He does when you pray.

The Father, the Word, and the Holy Ghost created the heavens and earth from nothing, this is evidence of the record of who we are; with the ability of God working through us as established from the beginning, not when the earth was formed but, in the beginning, when it was first thought of by God.

The Spirit confirms the truth of Christ in the earth, but the Holy Ghost states facts and details of the record documented in heaven.

1 John 5:8 states the witness in the earth is the spirit, the water, and the blood. Remember when the Lord began to create the earth His spirit moved upon the waters. This is a wonderful link between the creation of the heavens and the earth with creation of us becoming a new creature created by the shed blood sacrifice of its creator, Jesus.

> *Therefore if any man be in Christ, he is a new creature: old things are passed away; behold, all things are become new.*
>
> *(2 Corinthians 5:17)*

The *Holy Spirit* teaches us the knowledge of God by divine revelation and inspiration. The knowledge of God is not knowing about Him; it is the knowledge that God has.

During this time of transition from the natural to the spiritual, the following scripture is ever more important as we come into the knowledge that God Is.

> *But the Comforter, which is the Holy Ghost, whom the Father will send in my name, He shall teach you all things, and bring all things to your remembrance, whatsoever I have said unto you.*
>
> *(John 14:26)*

> *But when the Comforter is come, whom I will send unto you from the Father, even the Spirit of truth, which proceedeth from the Father, He shall testify of me: (Jesus)*
>
> *(John 15:26)*

The Bible is full of patterns and types to help us gain understanding of the Father, Son, and Holy Spirit. Patterns and types are at times shown through the stories in the Bible, which gives pictures of hidden meanings that link to the mystery of our relationship to God through the Godhead (Father, Son, Holy Spirit).

We must realize the Bible is able to reveal the plan of God and open our spiritual understanding which supports the reality of His existence.

Exodus is the book of the Bible that details the experiences the people of God had as they escaped the bondage of Egypt. A type of us escaping the world by acceptance of Christ.

I will use the following scriptures to illustrate how the Lord used a type to help us gain understanding.

> *Now the priest of Midian had seven daughters: and they came and drew water; and filled the troughs to water their father's flock.*
>
> *And the shepherds came and drove them away: but Moses stood up and helped them and watered their flock.*
>
> *And when they came to Reuel their father; he said, How is it that ye are come so soon today?*
>
> *And they said, An Egyptian delivered us out of the hand of the shepherds, and also drew water enough for us, and watered the flock.*
>
> *And he said unto his daughters, And were is he? Why is it ye have left the man? Call him, that he may eat bread.*
>
> *And Moses was content to dwell with the man: and he gave Moses Zipporah his daughter.*
>
> *(Exodus 2:16-21)*

"Reuel was the priest of Midian. Priest in verse 16 means one officiating as priest. Midian means strife or contention." (Strong's Expanded Exhaustive Concordance)

Therefore, Reuel (the friend of God) was the officiating priest over strife and contention as illustrated by the shepherds preventing the daughters from watering the flock. This act by the shepherds helps us to see a picture of the strife and contention of the world today played out through selfishness and self-gratification.

God the Father (Jehovah-self existent) has been doing very much the same thing since the beginning of creation. He has officiated the events and activities of this world through all its strife and contention.

Reuel has a second name; Jethro (Exodus 3:1) which means pre-eminence. Reuel / Jethro can be viewed as a type or illustration of God our Father.

The daughters said, "an Egyptian delivered us out of the hands of the shepherds." Moses was not an Egyptian (symbol of the world), but his outward appearance and dress made him appear as one. Much like Jesus was clothed in sinful flesh (as a mortal man), but He was deity, a part of the Godhead. This makes Moses a type of Jesus.

The word water in verse 16 is the Hebrew word shaqah. Strong's Concordance references two other words in conjunction with shaqah; they are shakar and shathah.

Shakar means to be filled with drink, to become tipsy and shathah means to imbibe (to receive into the mind and retain).

Let's see how this correlates with Acts chapter two.

> *Cretes and Arabians, we do hear them speak in our tongues the wonderful works of God.*
> *And they were all amazed, and were in doubt, saying one to another, What meaneth this?*

> *Others mocking said, These men are full of*
> *new wine.*
>
> *(Acts 2:11-13)*

The people who witnessed the infilling of the Holy Ghost for those present at the day of Pentecost observed the people being tipsy, appearing to be drunk on the spirit of God as He imbibed them filling their minds and soul with the Holy Ghost as they spoke in foreign languages they had not learned, enabling all the people to hear what was being said in their own language. This great event could not be rationalized as not being significant.

This describes the living water Jesus spoke of in John 4:10 and John 4:13-14. Water that when you drink it you never thirst again. Water that is a well springing up into everlasting life, *Glory to His Name!* Becoming born of the water and the spirit.

> *Jesus answered, Verily, verily, I say unto thee,*
> *Except a man be born of water and of the Spirit,*
> *he cannot enter into the kingdom of God.*
>
> *(John 3:5)*

The three witnesses in the earth (spirit, water, and the blood). Is illustrated here being born of the water and spirit through the sacrifice (blood) of Jesus Christ.

It appears the daughters are watering their fathers flock, but there is much more. Moses standing up to help the seven daughters when the shepherds drove them away from the living waters, illustrated Jesus as mediator for the church (the daughters) not only between mankind and God but also mankind and the under shepherds.

> *For there are certain men crept in unawares, who*
> *were before of old ordained to this condemnation,*
> *ungodly men, turning the grace of our God into*
> *lasciviousness, and denying the only Lord God,*
> *and our Lord Jesus Christ.*
>
> > *(Jude 1:4)*

Lasciviousness is the disposition of a soul without remorse, having no restraint. This was the state of some during the time when Jude wrote this communication about this condition being present in the church.

There must have been a belief that once you believed in Christ that your conversation and actions were covered by the blood of Jesus and therefore you didn't have to show restraint or guilt about the things you were doing. While persuading others to do the same.

The daughters symbolize the church as mentioned in Revelations 1:20 (the seven churches). The word daughter in these verses mean branch. Jesus referred to those who were His disciples as branches in John 15:5.

> *That the God of our Lord Jesus Christ, the Father*
> *of glory; may give unto you the spirit of wisdom*
> *and revelation in the knowledge of him:*
> > *The eyes of your understanding being*
> *enlightened; that ye may know what is the hope*

> *of his calling, and what the riches of the glory of*
> *his inheritance in the saints,*
>
> *And what is the exceeding greatness of his*
> *power to us-ward who believe, according to the*
> *working of his mighty power;*
>
> *(Ephesians 1:17-19)*

God Is! He has given us illustration after illustration in His Word of what He has done for us.

As I mentioned a few pages ago in the discussion about the daughters of Reuel tending his flock, which was linked to living water that was able to change the soul through the new thoughts that were generated and acted on from the heart because of the influence of the Holy Ghost; God brought organization and structure to our lives as His Spirit moves within us.

I always looked at baptism from a symbolic view of the death, burial, and resurrection into Jesus Christ. My understanding has been changed.

Water is the key substance to our physical make up accounting for 60% of our body. As God moved on the water with His Spirit dispensing His creative ability; likewise, as with us the creative ability of the Holy Ghost is used to create us a new.

Baptism is the outward show naturally to testify of your belief in Christ. Once we are born of the spirit and the water the creative ability of God is released in us through every cell and organ of our body.

This is how miraculous healing occurs, being mixed with our faith. Where the spirit of God is; there is liberty.

On the day of Pentecost, they were in one accord in one place as Jesus had told them they would soon be filled with the Holy Ghost (Acts 1:5).

Just as God moved upon the face of the deep, He also moves in the depths of the souls of men by His Spirit using the Word to create with in our hearts the substance of becoming a new creature in Christ (in the Word) 2 Corinthians 5:17.

Water is used to hydrate the body, a very key element to survival. The spirit works the same way. It is hydration for the soul and inner man. This links us to the life of God. A life where the impossible becomes possible and the unthinkable becomes reality.

Paul said, "my speech was not with enticing words of man's wisdom, but with the demonstration of the Spirit and of power." His faith was in the power of God. He did not speak the wisdom of the world to them. He spoke the wisdom of God in a mystery, the hidden wisdom, which God ordained before the world unto our glory (1 Corinthians 2:4-8). This mystery is Christ and Him being crucified.

Christ opens the ability to understand all the proprietorship (the right of owning) what God has provided.

Seek and you shall find deliverance from every bondage and stress that hinders you. Let the anointing (Greek word Chrisma) endow you with the Holy Spirit, enabling you to possess the knowledge and ability from God. Knowing when things get tough you know where your help comes from.

> *Seeing then that we have a great high priest, that*
> *is passed into the heavens, Jesus the Son of God,*
> *let us hold fast our profession.*
>
> *For we have not an high priest which cannot*
> *be touched with the feeling of our infirmities;*
> *but was in all points tempted like as we are, yet*
> *without sin.*
>
> *Let us therefore come boldly unto the throne*
> *of grace, that we may obtain mercy, and find*
> *grace to help in time of need.*
>
> *(Hebrews 4:14-16)*

The Godhead is an image of what we should be. Having the attributes of the father, the son, and the holy spirit.

> *At that day ye shall know that I am in my Father,*
> *and ye in me, and I in you.*
>
> *(John 14:20)*

When you acknowledge Jesus as Lord and are filled with the Holy Ghost. You become a new creature endowed with the power of God based on the record established in heaven.

*tr**u**th*

The Senses

The body receives external stimulus through the faculties of sight, smell, hearing, taste, and touch (our senses).

As baby's grow, they learn a lot through touch, taste, and smell. That is why when they see something, they smell it, touch it, then proceed to put it in their mouth.

The main two senses that impacts our belief system and actions as adults are seeing and hearing.

> *And when the woman saw that the tree was good*
> *for food, and that it was pleasant to the eyes, and*
> *a tree to be desired to make one wise, she took of*
> *the fruit thereof, and did eat, and gave also unto*
> *her husband with her; and he did eat.*
>
> *(Genesis 3:6)*

What Eve saw and heard played a large role in her decision-making process to eat or not to eat the fruit on the tree.

The function of eating is presented along with seeing, hearing, and smelling as a basic function of living. These basic functions influenced Eve to take the fruit of the knowledge of good and evil. Her senses enticed her to partake, and the thought that she would gain knowledge that would make her like God was an extra benefit.

Think of Adam and Eve without thoughts, knowledge, nor experience with cunning, ignorance, or shame.

> *And they heard the voice of the Lord God walking in the garden in the cool of the day: and Adam and his wife hid themselves from the presence of the Lord God amongst the trees of the garden.*
>
> *And the Lord God called unto Adam and said unto him, Where art thou?*
>
> *And he said, I heard thy voice in the garden, and I was afraid, because I was naked; and I hid myself.*
>
> *(Genesis 3:8-10)*

Their actions gave them the capability to think in a separated and defeated realm away from God. They learned fear and their vocabulary increased with words like afraid and naked.

Can you imagine never having thoughts that are lower than the realm of the Lord's goodness and capability. Where fear, doubt, and unbelief never occur.

The senses benefit us in our natural environment. But have little value when it comes to helping us define and understand the things in the spiritual realm.

Finally, brethren, whatsoever things are true, whatsoever things are honest, whatsoever things are just, whatsoever things are pure, whatsoever things are lovely, whatsoever things are of good report; if there be any virtue, and if there be any praise, think on these things.

(Philippians 4:8)

The mind is the battle ground. We must change our pattern of thoughts. Everything we sense through our five senses (see, smell, hear, touch, taste) is processed through our mind. Prior experience guides us to make conclusions as we interpret what our senses are communicating to us; these conclusions can limit God. We must unlearn the fallen nature and embrace our new nature.

And be not conformed to this world: but be ye transformed by the renewing of your mind, that ye may prove what is that good, and acceptable, and perfect will of God.

(Romans 12:2)

We must renew our minds to get back to the state of mind and life that Adam had before he experienced the ability to think and act contrary to God.

To understand that "God Is" we must come to the realization that God's Word is truth and understand our linkage to the celestial.

> *There are also celestial bodies, and bodies terrestrial: but the glory of the celestial is one, and the glory of the terrestrial is another.*
>
> (1 Corinthians 15:40)

> *Are they not all ministering spirits, sent forth to minister for them who shall be heirs of salvation?*
>
> (Hebrews 1:14)

A celestial body is anything in the heavenlies and terrestrial bodies are anything on earth. We cannot see angels with our eyes; we cannot hear conversations that are happening in the heavenlies. At times we cannot hear when God is speaking to us through the spirit as individuals. But the above scripture let us know that angels are here to minister for us and help us in times of need.

I was traveling to my Mom's with my oldest daughter one evening during the winter and I hit a patch of black ice. The truck began to spin with ditches on both sides of the highway.

I used driving skills and training. Turning into the direction of the spin but it got worse and we were traveling toward the ditch on the left side of the road.

I let go of the steering wheel and raised my hands and said, "Lord Jesus help your child."

The truck spun around and backed onto a strip of dirt that covered the ditch on the right side of the road just wide enough for the truck to fit. Have you ever seen a vehicle back in a straight line for about 30 feet while it was in a spin? That day I knew for sure that there were ministering spirits that help us and the following scripture became a reality to me.

> *For he shall give his angels charge over thee, to*
> *keep thee in all thy ways.*
>
> *(Psalms 91:11)*

I believe an angel directed my truck that day to protect my daughter and me.

The natural man is limited to the realm of creation, but the spiritual man has endless capabilities.

We must walk by faith and not by site!

> *And when the servant of the man of God was*
> *risen early, and gone forth, behold, an host*
> *compassed the city both with horses and chariots.*
> *And his servant said unto him, Alas, my master!*
> *How shall we do?*
>
> *And he answered, Fear not: for they that be*
> *with us are more than they that be with them.*
>
> *And Elisha prayed, and said, Lord, I pray*
> *thee, open his eyes, that he may see. And the Lord*
> *opened the eyes of the young man; and he saw:*
> *and, behold, the mountain was full of horses and*
> *chariots of fire round about Elisha.*
>
> *(2 Kings 6:15-17)*

We must believe that God is with us and He will never forsake us even if we do not see it.

God established light visible to the human eye (Genesis 1:14-15). The visible spectrum is the portion of an electromagnetic spectrum that can be seen by the human eye. Electromagnetic radiation in this range of wavelengths is called visible light or simply light. The visible light spectrum is a series of colors: *red, orange, yellow, green, blue, indigo, and violet.* Each color corresponds to a different wavelength of light.

The rainbow illustrated the proof of this. When light from the sun shines through or reflects off water after the rain. We are able the see the spectrum of colors in the sky.

This is all a part of the creation of physics as I mentioned in "Truth 3 – Resolution for Darkness."

Light travels at 186,000 miles per second. It is the media that allows us to see objects, color, and shapes. So, why could not the servant see the angels. Because the angels where not in the realm of the terrestrial where light could illuminate the spectrum of colors to make them visible. Items on earth has molecules that are visible to light at 186,000 miles per second allowing us to see them.

Angels are celestial and operate in the spirit realm; therefore, they do not have a molecular structure and more than likely do no operate slower than the speed of light. I believe this is the reason angels cannot be seen.

Light enables us to see in the natural. Just as being enlightened spiritually allows us to see the victory over spiritual conditions of ignorance, death, and destruction creating a life filled with peace and inspiration.

Hearing God is different from hearing sound in our terrestrial environment. It is having an ear to hear what the spirit of the Lord has to say.

And the Lord called yet again, Samuel. And Samuel arose and went to Eli, and said, Here am I; for thou didst call me. And he answered, I called not, my son; lie down again.

Now Samuel did not yet know the Lord, neither was the word of the Lord yet revealed unto him.

And the Lord called Samuel again the third time. And he arose and went to Eli, and said, Here am I; for thou didst call me. And Eli perceived that the Lord had called the child.

Therefore, Eli said unto Samuel, Go, lie down: and it shall be, if he call thee, that thou shalt say, Speak, Lord; for thy servant heareth. So, Samuel went and lay down in his place.

And the Lord came, and stood, and called as at the other times, Samuel, Samuel. Then Samuel answered, Speak; for thy servant heareth.

(1 Samuel 3:6-10)

Verse seven is the key. Even though Samuel had ministered before the Lord and served Eli the priest. Yet, he did not know God nor did he have a revelation of the Word of God (God's Word uncovered enabling understanding).

I love this scripture because it points to the need to have a revelation of Jesus Christ (the Word) to be able to interact with God. Through interaction is how we come to know Him through observation. As we interact with God, we begin to think about those interactions, which help us to gain experience communicating and understanding how he leads us.

Some of us are in the same state as Samuel. Going to church and helping the pastor with events and programs but do not truly know God and do not have a revelation of the Word (Jesus Christ).

Sound travels at a speed of 767 miles per hour. So, anything traveling slower that 767 miles per hour we hear it almost instantly.

Then when an object travels faster than 767 miles per hour, we hear it after it has already passed us. At times this is how we are when it comes to hearing the Lord. We hear at a future date after the message has already been delivered. This is like Samuel's experience. How long would it have taken him to gain understanding, without the instruction from Eli helping him to open the dialogue so the message God wanted to give could be communicated.

> *Also, I heard the voice of the Lord, saying, Whom shall I send, and who will go for us? Then said I, Here am I; send me.*
>
> *And he said, Go, and tell this people, Hear ye indeed, but understand not; and see ye indeed, but perceive not.*

> *Make the heart of this people fat, and make their ears heavy, and shut their eyes; lest they see with their eyes, and hear with their ears, and understand with their heart, and convert, and be healed.*
>
> *(Isaiah 6:8-10)*

To hear the Lord, we must seek Him and respond to His call as Samuel and Isaiah did. Then when the still small voice speaks your soul and heart are sensitive to the sound of His voice.

We must be able to ignore distractions to be able to listen to the Lord. The key is what do you do after you hear His voice speaking to our inner soul. At times God's voice is representative of a thought we may have had.

> *And he said, Go forth, and stand upon the mount before the Lord. And, behold, the Lord passed by, and a great and strong wind rent the mountains, and brake in pieces the rocks before the Lord; but the Lord was not in the wind: and after the wind an earthquake; but the Lord was not in the earthquake:*
>
> *And after the earthquake a fire; but the Lord was not in the fire; and after the fire a still small voice.*
>
> *And it was so, when Elijah heard it, that he wrapped his face in his mantle, and went out, and stood in the entering of the cave. And, behold*

> *there came a voice unto him, and said, What*
> *doest thou here, Elijah?*
>
> > *(1 Kings 19:11-13)*

Notice after the Lord passed by in the verse above wind, earthquake, and fire preceded the voice of God; all three are elements of the terrestrial (of the earth we live in). Then the voice of the Lord spoke. Don't be distracted, have a ear to hear.

Elijah's name and where he was born is a great indicator of the will of God for us. His name means God is Jehovah. He was a Tishbite (meaning born in Tishbe). Tisbite[30] means recourse a source of help providing alternative solutions.

Our Lord the great Jehovah the eternal all-knowing wants to be our source to provide solutions in our lives.

We are spiritual beings with a need to commune with our Father in heaven. Strive to hear His voice. He spoke after all the earthly distractions were finished.

Find your secret place and commune with God.

The key for us is to have a spiritual eye and possess the ability to hear and know when God is speaking.

t r u t h 6

Patterns and Types

I have shared the pattern of the mercy seat in "Truth 1", when I discussed the scriptures in Exodus chapter 25.

In this "Truth" I will discuss the kingdoms of the earth. You will see God's capability to link prophecy to actual life events that happened. Prophecy is used to help us see spiritual meaning of those same events in a historical context.

These reoccurring patterns and types help us to have confidence and faith in the Word of God.

World events seem to just happen without guidance from anyone. This is not true!

I discussed the kingdoms of the earth in a prior work (What Must Come to Pass) to illustrate the fulfillment of God's prophetic plan in the earth.

I will use some of the realities from scriptures to show the existence of an overall plan detailed 600 years before Christ in a dream that is and has been executed throughout history.

This validates that "God Is"; since every word has been executed authenticating Him as the author of the present and the future.

God orchestrates the events of the earth and puts leaders in place to ensure His Word will be accomplished.

> *For promotion cometh neither from the east, nor from the west, nor from the south.*
>
> *But God is the judge: he putteth down one, and setteth up another.*
>
> *(Psalms 75:6-7)*

The origin and source of revealing the plan of the Lord for how the kingdoms of the earth will progress until the time of the return of Christ occurs in Daniel 2:29-35. Daniel's interpretation of the dream is documented in verse 36 through 45.

> *Daniel answered and said, Blessed be the name of God forever and ever: for wisdom and might are his:*
>
> *And he changeth the times and the seasons: he removeth kings, and setteth up kings: he giveth wisdom unto the wise, and knowledge to them that knows understanding:*
>
> *He revealeth the deep and secret things: he knoweth what is in the darkness, and the light dwelleth with him.*
>
> *(Daniel 2:20-22)*

There are five periods of world government illustrated by the image shown to Nebuchadnezzar in the dream. Babylon the head of gold from 609 before Christ (BC) to 539 BC; Persia the breast and arms of silver from 539 BC to 331 BC; Greece the belly and thighs of brass from 331 BC to 168 BC; Rome the legs of iron from 168 BC – 476 AD (anno Domini – the year of our Lord) which was the government in control during the life of Christ. Then there was the feet and toes of iron and clay.

And whereas thou sawest the feet and toes, part of potters clay; and part of iron, the kingdom shall be divided; but there shall be in it the strength of the iron mixed with the miry clay.

And as the toes of the feet were part of iron, and part of clay, so the kingdom shall be partly strong, and partly broken.

And whereas thou sawest iron mixed with miry clay, they shall mingle themselves with the seed of men; but they shall not cleave on to another, even as the iron is not mixed with the clay.

(Daniel 2:41-43)

The feet and toes at the foundation of the image represents more than the dividing of the Roman Empire; they represent the final ten-nation alliance with its complexity by the mingling and mixing of multiple nations and cultures. Yet the influence of Rome will still be present as signified by the iron being mingled with the clay.

This is not like the empires of the past, which had a central dominate figure. This will be the world leadership of the end time constructed of alliances between multiple leaders.

> *And in the days of these kings shall the God of heaven set up a kingdom; which shall never be destroyed: and the kingdom shall not be left to other people, but it shall break in pieces and consume all these kingdoms, and it shall stand forever.*
>
> *Forasmuch as thou sawest that the stone was cut out of the mountain without hands, and that it brake in pieces the iron, the brass, the clay, the silver, and the gold; the great God hath made known to the king what shall come to pass here after: and the dream is certain, and the interpretation thereof sure.*
>
> *(Daniel 2:44-45)*

Christ is the rock cut from the mountain of God that will smash this current world system and government ruled by men. As I discussed it has been God's plan from the foundations of the world to defeat darkness and establish His kingdom at the end of this current age.

We will transition from the government of man to the Messiah ruling the earth.

There are no stronger illustrations that "God Is" than the fulfillment of the dream as Daniel interpreted it to be. This dream has been fulfilled until the time in which we live. The time of toes and iron and clay. There is no doubt in my mind that God Is and is the orchestrator of the history of the earth.

The Bible is full of patterns that work to clarify God's influences from beginning to end. The Lord used patterns and types (forms and models as imitations by using a person or thing to foreshadow or represent another person or thing) to help us gain understanding.

An example of patterns and types is the feast system Passover, Unleavened Bread, First Fruits, Weeks (Pentecost), Trumpets, Day of Atonement, Tabernacles (Booths). These feasts illustrate the plan for mans redemption and his future in eternity.

Just as Nebuchadnezzar's dream showed the natural progression of man's government the feast system shows the progression of God's plan for the deliverance and preparation of mankind for eternity.

The feasts are laid out in the book of Leviticus chapter 23. The Jewish calendar month typically crosses from the middle of one months to the middle of the next month on our calendar. The months of the Jewish calendar are Nisan, Iyar, Sivan, Tammuz, Av, Elul, Tishrei, Cheshvan, Kislev, Tevet, Shevat, and Adar.

The first month on the Jewish calendar is the month of Nisan (March-April). Notice that the first seven months of the calendar are aligned with the feast system and the feast system is the pattern and type for the salvation of man and the completion of the fullness of days (the revealing of the New Jerusalem with the new heaven and earth).

The feasts occur in the first seven months just as God created the heavens and the earth in six days and rested on the seventh. These are correlated together proving the illustration of the pattern that has been established for man's salvation. Remember Adam the perfect man was created on day seven and so it shall be for the people of God entering the rest of God on day seven of the existence of mankind after 6000 years. Remember a1000 years in the Lord's sight is just as if yesterday had past (Psalms 91:4). 6000 years is equivalent to six days in the realm of God.

Four of the feasts have been fulfilled Passover, Unleavened Bread, First Fruits, and the feast of Weeks (Pentecost).

Passover was initiated when the children of Israel were in Egypt and the plague of the first born was issued in the land. The people of Israel were instructed to kill a lamb and put the blood on the door post. By doing so the plague passed over their homes and family.

Jesus was the Passover lamb sacrificed for our sins.

The feast of Unleavened Bread illustrates the exit of Israel from Egypt. Which is linked to the burial of Christ the bread of life, which provided for our sanctification and deliverance from the world.

The feast of First Fruits of the barley harvest was the resurrection of Jesus the first to be resurrected from death.

Fifty days later was the feast of Weeks (Pentecost) the beginning of the wheat harvest. This was fulfilled in Acts chapter two when the Believers where filled with the Holy Ghost and a harvest of three thousand men were saved.

The last three feast (Trumpets, Atonement, and Tabernacles) have not been fulfilled yet. These last three feast all occur within the same month of Tishrel on the Jewish calendar (see Leviticus 23:24-34).

The feast of Trumpets (September/October) at the beginning to the seventh month signals the return of Jesus (1 Thessalonians 4:13-18 / Revelations chapter eight through chapter ten).

The Day of Atonement on the 10th day of the month (Romans 11:25-28 / Revelations chapter 14). This is a period when repentance is practiced that the Lord may issue atonement for sin.

The feast of Tabernacles occurs on the 15th day of the month (Revelation 20:1-6); when we tabernacle with God for a thousand years (the seventh day of rest Genesis Chapter two) and then the new haven and earth are established.

If God can predict the kingdoms of the earth (Daniels interpretation of Nebuchadnezzar's dream) and put in place the spiritual events to take place (the feast system) thousands of years before they happen for a pattern / guide for sanctification and salvation of mankind. There is no doubt in my mind that there is a God and He exists.

t r u t h

Know Him

All things are delivered to me of my Father: and no man knoweth who the Son is, but the Father; and who the Father is, but the Son, and he to whom the Son will reveal him.

(Luke 10:22)

If we have seen the Son, we have seen the father. Jesus is the reflection of the Father.

To know someone, you must understand the attributes they possess. God is infinite, before all things, and in all things; immutable never changes; and has life within Himself.

These four names tell us how men in the Old Testament viewed God:

> El Elyon – God most high
>
> El Roi – God that sees
>
> El Shaddai – God Almighty
>
> Jehovah Jireh – God will provide

Inherent characteristics of the soul of mankind seeks to know the true God. There is something within us that reaches out at some point in our life and wonders if God exists. This may happen when we are young, or it may happen when we are adults.

> *Then Paul stood in the midst of Mars hill, and said, Ye men of Athens, I perceive that in all things ye are too superstitious.*
>
> *For as I passed by, and beheld your devotions, I found an altar with this inscription, TO THE UNKOWN GOD. Whom therefore ye ignorantly worship, him declare I unto you.*
>
> *God that made the world and all things therein, seeing that he is Lord of heaven and earth, dwelleth not in temples made with hands;*
>
> *Neither is worshipped with men's hands, as though he needed any thing, seeing he giveth to all life, and breath, and all things;*
>
> *And hath made of one blood all nations of men for to dwell on all the face of the earth, and hath determined the times before appointed, and the bounds of their habitation;*
>
> *That they should seek the Lord, if haply they might feel after him, and find him, though he be not far from every one of us:*
>
> (Acts 17:22-27)

These scriptures explain it perfectly. The worship of God and the ability to know Him is with in us. We must seek to find our relationship with Him through an internal assessment of ourselves. He is not far away.

> *Ask, and it shall be given you; seek, and ye shall find; knock, and it shall be opened unto you:*
>> *For every one that asketh receiveth; and he that seeketh findeth; and to him that knocketh it shall be opened.*
>
> *(Matthew 7:7-8)*

To know Him we must dwell in the secret place of the most-high and inquire in His temple. This means we must spend time in prayer, reading His Word, and then giving Him praise for His mighty acts as He reveals Himself to us.

This place is your hiding place; a place where we are covered and protected.

> *He that dwelleth in the secret place of the most High shall abided under the shadow of the Almighty.*
>> *I will say of the Lord, He is my refuge and my fortress: my God; in him will I trust.*
>
> *(Psalms 91:1-2)*

When you pray how do you know that the Lord hears you? The Holy Ghost is our comforter. He confirms it is done or he gives us peace through the ordeal.

Our personal beliefs influence our relationship, understanding, and interactions with God.

Our belief system is what determines how deep we go into a relationship with the Father. The relationship will be what we put into it.

Desires can drive us to make decisions and take paths that create uncertainty about the direction for our life. Especially if those desires do not line up with the will of God.

> *Trust in the Lord with all thine heart; and lean not unto thine own understanding.*
>   *In all thy ways acknowledge him, and he shall direct thy paths.*
>   *(Proverbs 3:5-6)*

As you acknowledge Him you then will begin to improve your relationship with Him and your knowledge of Him will grow as you are learning to be led by Him. As He leads you begin to understand how He interacts with you.

Through my life I have improved my listening skills and understand more now how God works in my life. I am still learning and expect to keep learning the rest of my life. You cannot put God in a template to determine His workings in our lives and the earth.

Sometimes waiting makes things clearer. My mom would say, "I am waiting on the Lord." Where I have always had the belief God will give favor mixed with His grace and I had no fear and was willing to make a change quickly. Maybe too quickly at times not giving God a chance to work. You know he works through people. And sometimes it takes a while for Him to get the people to line up to accomplish what He desires for you.

The earth is not going through random metamorphosis of evolving change. There is and always has been the model God has set for His purpose in this world.

As you have seen from the biblical illustrations, I have shared in Truth 6 (Patterns and Types). God uses events that occur in this world for his purpose.

Sometimes we must be unsettled to be able to listen to the master. Our nation had become a den of wolves lurking and prowling for an opportunity to place blame to make some look incompetent, while not even recognizing the good they do. This attribute of wanting to bring down one to exalt your own selfish objectives are not from God.

We ever learn but never come to the full knowledge of the truth (2 Timothy 3:7). Truth is the reality that is related to God.

God so loved the world that He gave His only begotten son, that none would perish. This is compassion!

When you know Him, you can sense and feel what He feels in many situations.

Our desire should be:

> *That ye might walk worthy of the Lord unto all pleasing, being fruitful in every good work, and increasing in the knowledge of God;*
> *(Colossians 1:10)*

To know Him is to know how and when He is acting in our lives to direct us in the paths, we should follow.

t r u t h

Interrelationship

> "Interrelationship is the way in which two or
> more things or people are connected and affect
> one another."

Our new beginning is through interaction with the Lord God using the communication link, we have through Christ and the Holy Spirit, creating the interrelationship between Him and us.

Then we will fully be able to discern how our actions affect the plans of the Lord and in turn what His responses are because of our actions.

God's responses are situational! It all depends on the path you chose. His promises are conditional.

> *After the number of the days in which ye searched*
> *the land, even forth days, each day for a year,*
> *shall ye bear your iniquities, even forty years, and*
> *ye shall know my breach of promise.*

> *I the Lord have said, I will surely do it unto*
> *all this evil congregation, that are gathered*
> *together against me: in this wilderness they shall*
> *be consumed, and there they shall die.*
>
> (Numbers 14:34-35)

There was a requirement of faith to act the children of Israel must perform to enter the promise land. They made excuses as for why they could not possess the land therefore, the Lord breached the promise and that generation died in the wilderness.

Discernment is recognizing the causes and effects of an action as we observe and reflect on what has happened. Are you able to discern why events occur in your life due to the interrelationship (cause and effect) with God.

Let us discuss three elements that influence an individual's belief or nonbelief for the existence of God and His interrelationship with us. Destructive weather, doubt that "God Is", and the inherent characteristic of mankind all influence a person's ultimate belief around the existence of God.

> *Because the creature itself also shall be delivered*
> *from the bondage of corruption into the glorious*
> *liberty of the children of God.*
>
> *For we know that the whole creation groaneth*
> *and travaileth in pain together until now.*
>
> (Romans 8:21-22)

The reason for the creation to groan and travail is the same reason many are pressing to find our way back to God; the failure of Adam caused disorder in the earth which generates natural disasters such as earthquakes, tornados, and hurricanes.

Some people think when these disasters occur that there is no God. They do not realize we live in a world that is experiencing birth pains. The pains of the revealing of the sons of God.

God operates in the realm of the unseen, but He is ever present. It is hard for some to believe that "God Is" because they cannot see Him. I see Him though His answers to prayer.

The inherent characteristics of the soul of man are influenced by the operation of a free will. Which confuses the issue of whether we can be saved when there is evidence each day of our free will in operation against the will of God.

> *I protest by your rejoicing which I have in Christ*
> *Jesus our Lord, I die daily.*
> (*1 Corinthians 15:31*)

We must strive daily to align with the Word of God and overcome the influence of unrighteousness.

When the Lord interacts in the affairs of our lives; what is our response? How do we define the events of the interaction? Do we feel we are being punished; do we think God does not care about us because this is happening; do we not assess what happened at all? We chalk it up simply as being a part of life.

I believe at times God does interact with the earth to protect us from disorder. Jesus spoke to the storm in Luke 8:24 and I believe He still does when His children cry out.

Storms, drought, hurricanes, tornados, and floods are not orchestrated by the hand of God. The creation is also in bondage groaning and travailing in pain.

Nature is now out of order when once upon a time it had never even rained on the earth (Genesis 2:5). Animals did not desire to kill each other they came together in peace to allow Adam to name them (Genesis 2:19). When the Lord returns it will be this way once again.

> *The wolf and the lamb shall feed together, and the lion shall eat straw like the bullock; and dust shall be the serpent's meat. They shall not hurt nor destroy in all my holy mountain, saith the Lord.*
> *(Isaiah 65:25)*

I am writing this work as the COVID-19 virus impacts the lives of many throughout the world.

I thought about how people are viewing the pestilence that has spread from country to country. It has proven how frail our world really is.

I have a few questions to ask:

Did you seek God for answers why? Did you pray for His intervention for the world? Did you wonder if satan authored this attack to inflict suffering on mankind or did you think in God's wisdom He allowed it to happen for a purpose that has not been revealed?

If COVID-19 is being used by God all we could do is seek His forgiveness and ask Him for protection.

Do you think this is occurring for the Lord to shape the world organization in some fashion to establish future occurrences of His will? An example of this is the plagues of Egypt that Moses communicated to Pharaoh.

In the past destruction caused people to wake up and realize "God Is". He is still truly in control and is more than able to help us, only if we call on Him out of a sincere heart.

At the start of the virus I touched and agreed with the President when he said, "I am hopeful that it will begin to decline by spring."

I also, prayed to God to make it so! My reason was that God is compassionate, He acts on faith, and the President is the leader of our nation and he had thoughts of good and an expected outcome.

So on March eighteenth I sent a text to some of my family members. Telling them about Psalms 91 and encurraging them that in the coming weeks there would be an improvement in the rate of infection and that there would be more tests to overcome in the future.

Three weeks later the rate of infection had begun to level off and a downward trend had started. This was something allowed by God, but not necessarily orchestrated by God.

We have seen a second challenge in our nation concerning race relations just a few weeks after the COVID-19 infections improved.

We as believers must seek God to understand the complexity and motives behind some requests for change.

Protest and rioting were deemed as necessary to allow years of frustration to be released as a mental health need. With no mention of the need to continue the CDC rules for distancing. Yet, churches and others with different views were forced to continue the CDC rules and lawfully prosecuted if found disobeying the rules. This seems to be an effort to allow certain views to be propagated.

In times like these we need **interrelationship** with God to help us discern the current events!

The inability to see God working in our lives is twofold. Our insensitivity and our inability to define characteristics within events and their intended expected outcomes hinders the truth from being revealed.

Our inability to envision what has already been established in heaven stops us from moving forward to obtain what the Lord has provisioned for us.

When events happen that challenge our belief system; we enter a period where the spiritual truth is harder to discover because of the reality being played out in front of us.

In 1 Chronicles chapter 21 David wanted to number the people. In chapter 20 Israel had been in war after war so David wanted to know how many people they had.

Did David do this because he thought there was strength in numbers? But his servant Joab asked why this do, are not all the people his servants; but David insisted.

In verse seven of chapter 21 the Bible said, "that God smote Israel because He was displeased."

David admits to God he had done wrong but that did not stop the judgement of God. In verse ten God sends Gad to tell David to choose one of three things for God to do as punishment.

> *So Gad came to David, and said unto him, Thus saith the Lord, Choose thee*
>
> *Either three years famine; or three months to be destroyed before thy foes, while that the sword of thine enemies overtaketh thee; or else three days the sword of the Lord, even the pestilence, in the land, and the angel of the Lord destroying throughout all the coasts of Israel. Now therefore advise thyself what word I shall bring again to him that sent me.*
>
> *And David said unto Gad, I am in a great strait: let me fall now into the hand of the Lord; for very great are his mercies: but let me not fall into the hand of man.*
>
> *So the Lord sent pestilence upon Israel: and there fell of Israel seventy thousand men.*
>
> *And God sent an angel unto Jerusalem to destroy it: and as he was destroying, the Lord beheld, and he repented him of the evil, and said to the angel that destroyed, It is enough, stay now thine hand. And the angel of the Lord stood by the threshingfloor of Ornan the Jebusite.*

> *And David lifted up his eyes, and saw the*
> *angel of the Lord stand between the earth and*
> *the heaven, having a drawn sword in his hand*
> *stretched out over Jerusalem. Then David and the*
> *elders of Israel, who were clothed in sackcloth, fell*
> *upon their faces.*
>
> *And David said unto God, Is it not I that*
> *commanded the people to be numbered? Even I*
> *it is that have sinned and done evil indeed; but*
> *as for these sheep, what have they done? Let thine*
> *hand, I pray thee, O Lord my God, be on me, and*
> *on my father's house; but not on thy people, that*
> *they should be plagued.*
>
> *(1 Chronicles 21:11-17)*

Please note the reason why the angel stood by the threshingfloor[31]. Threshing is by using a tool to trample or tread out the wheat to smooth it out. The fact the angel was seen there tells us the Lord was using the pestilence and the destruction brought on by the angel to help the people know the results of disobedience there by smoothing out the unwanted particles that separate us from God.

God's interaction with David after he disobeyed by numbering the people, has all the signs of a true interrelationship (our connection to God with its cause and effect relationships).

He interacted with David to the point of choosing his own punishment. David realized his actions impacted the people of

God; as shown in verse 17 when he asked what have the sheep (God's flock) done.

This illustration shows how events in our personal lives can be orchestrated by the Lord; for our good, for our correction, or for our development.

In either case will you be willing to fall on your face and seek God for answers?

As we learn to interpret the events that are happening, you must not lean to your understanding but acknowledge God that he may direct you through the challenge.

When the children of Israel camped at the Jordan river before they passed over the Lord gave instruction that they should follow.

Some of us have not experienced or traveled this road of assessing the events of life and asking the Lord for guidance around the spiritual implications as we learn about our interrelationship with the Lord, we must understand how this is established with Him. Many times, we pray and act in a reactive mode.

> *And it came to pass after three days, that the officers went through the host;*
>
> *And they commanded the people, saying, When ye see the ark of the covenant of the Lord your God, and the priests the Levites bearing it, then ye shall remove from your place, and go after it.*

> *Yet there shall be a space between you and it, about two thousand cubits by measure: come not near unto it, that ye may know the way by which ye must go: <u>for ye have not passed this way heretofore</u>.*
>
> *And Joshua said unto the people, Sanctify yourselves: for to morrow the Lord will do wonders among you.*
>
> *(Joshua 3:2-5)*

Following the ark is an illustration of the Lord's guidance. In the times we live in we must gain answers of the origin and purpose of the challenges in life and how we are to handle them; this is only available through Christ. By the way Joshua means Jesus in the Greek.

Let the Lord lead you in the coming years along the road of your journey as you experience His promises.

> *Humble yourselves therefore under the mighty hand of God, that he may exalt you in due time.*
>
> *Casting all your care upon him, for he careth for you.*
>
> *Be sober, be vigilant; because your adversary the devil, as a roaring lion, walketh about, seeking whom he may devour:*
>
> *Whom resist stedfast in the faith, knowing that the same afflictions are accomplished in your brethren that are in the world.*

> *But the God of all grace, who hath called us unto his eternal glory by Christ Jesus, after that ye have suffered a while, make you perfect, stablish, strengthen, settle you.*
>
> *To him be glory and dominion for ever and ever. Amen.*
>
> *(1 Peter 5:6-11)*

Life will not be without afflictions. Some driven by the devil to defeat you; some events are allowed by God to help develop you; to build your faith and relationship with Him.

Always assess the events of your life.

> *But we glory in tribulations also: knowing that tribulation worketh patience;*
>
> *And patience, experience; and experience, hope:*
>
> *(Romans5:3-4)*

Experience[32] in this verse means the process of proving. God uses trials, viruses, disasters for us to see our response and then grow from what we have experienced.

The key to our new beginning is understanding how our actions affect the interrelationship with God.

> *If I shut up heaven that there be no rain; or if I command the locusts to devour the land, or if I send pestilence among my people;*

> *If my people, which are called by my name,*
> *shall humble themselves, and pray, and seek my*
> *face, and turn from their wicked ways; then will*
> *I hear from heaven, and will heal their land.*
> *Now mine eyes shall be open, and mine ears*
> *attend unto the prayer that is made in this place.*
> *(2 Chronicles 7:13-15)*

Our relationships with God are situational/conditional. There is truly an interrelationship between us and God. We are connected, our actions affect His actions and His actions influence ours.

Epilogue

This work has given the rationale for the creation and God's efforts to reveal darkness that we may walk in light.

Through understanding we come to know the relationships between us and the Godhead (father, son, holy spirit).

The ability to see the acts of God in your life has been enhanced while recognizing the need to improve listening skills through seeking the Lord in prayer have been illustrated through this work.

The patterns and types given in the Bible shows the establishment of world leaders past and future to fulfill the plan of God. These plans (for world leaders) run congruently with the plans for the spiritual development of God's people as illustrated through the feast system. Culminating in the return of Christ.

We are now going through the process of learning to know God and how our interrelationship to Him works.

This work establishes the basic premise that "God Is" through showing how His plans were revealed through the scriptures thousands of years before the actual events happen.

Providing the evidence that:

> *(The earth is the Lord's, and the fulness thereof;*
> *the world, and they that dwell therein.*
> *For he hath founded it upon the seas, and*
> *established it upon the floods.*
>
> *Psalms 24:1-2)*

Bibliography

Holman Bible Publishing, Giant Print Reference Bible (King James Version), Nashville, Tennessee, 1996.

James Strong, LLD, STD, "The new Strong's Expanded Exhaustive Concordance" of the Bible (Red Letter Edition), Nashville, TN: Thomas Nelson Publishers, 2010

About the Author

The author has enjoyed forty years as a child of the King.

In May of 2005 completed the requirements to receive a Master of Arts degree in "Biblical Studies.

Has served the church in the following capacity: men's leader for Sunday Bible Study, men's group leader, and youth Sunday School leader (ages-14-18).

Had the opportunity to minister for congregations in Oklahoma, Texas, Missouri, and Louisiana.

Self-published three other works: Creation of the Glorious Church, What Must Come to Pass, and Insights for Believers.

Believes in the words Jesus said while giving an example of how to pray.

> *Thy kingdom come; Thy will be done in earth, as it is in heaven.*
>
> *(Matthew 6:10)*

Appendix

All scripture references were taken from The Holy Bible: King James Version, Holman Bible Publishing, Nashville, Tennessee, 1996.

DEADICATION
Ephesians 1:17-19;

EPIGRAPH
Hebrews 11:6

PREFACE
Psalms 91:1-2

INTRODUCTION
John 4:24; **Luke** 10:22; **Revelation** 1:8; **Exodus** 3:13-14; 6:3; **Genesis** 22:17; 27:36; 27:15-30; **Galatians** 4:6; **Jeremiah** 1:5; **John** 3:15; **Romans** 8:21-25;

CREATION RATIONALE
Genesis 3:15; 1:26; 6:2; **Luke** 10:18; **Ezekiel** 28:14-15; 28:13; 28:16-17; **Exodus** 25:18-20; **1 John** 3:8; **Revelation** 12:10; 12:7-9; 12:13; 21:1-2; **Hebrews** 4:12-13; **John** 4:24;

UNDERSTANDING
Genesis 4:1-5; 4:8; 4:16; **Proverbs** 8:14; 8:22-30; 9:10; 4:7; **Isaiah** 42:5-9; **Revelations** 4:11 **John** 5:4-5; **Colossians** 2:2-3; **1 John** **5:4-5**

RESOLUTION For DARKNESS
Genesis 1:1-5; 1:14-19; 2:7; **John** 1:4-5; **Acts** 2:2-4; **Psalms** 24:1-5; **1 Peter** 2:9; **2 Peter** 1:19

FATHER, SON, HOLY SPIRIT
Genesis 1:26; **Exodus** 2:16-21; **Psalms** 27:4-8; **Isaiah** 6:8-10; **Matthew** 6:7-8; **John** 4:24; 14:26; 15:26; 3:5; 14:20; **1 Corinthians** 2:14; **Hebrews** 4:12-13; 4:14-16; **Ephesians** 1:17-19; **1 John** 1:1-5; 5:7-8; **Jude** 1:4; **2 Corinthians** 5:17

SENSES
Genesis 3:6; 3:8-10; **1 Samuel** 3:6-10; **1 Kings** 19:11-13; **2 Kings** 6:15-17; **Psalms** 91:11; **Romans** 12:2; **1 Corinthians** 15:40; **Hebrews** 1:14; **Philippians** 4:8

PATTERNS AND TYPES
Psalms 75:6-7; **Daniel** 2:20-22; 2:41-43; 2:44-45

KNOW HIM

Matthew 7:7-8; **Luke** 10:22; **Acts** 17:22:27; **Psalms** 91:1-2; **Proverbs** 3:5-6; **Colossians** 1:10

INTERRELATIONSHIP

Romans 8:21-22; **1 Corinthians** 15:31; **Isaiah** 65:25; **1 Chronicles** 21:11-17; **Joshua** 3:2-5; **1 Peter** 5:6-11; **Romans** 5:3-4; **2 Chronicles** 7:13-15

EPILOGUE

Psalms 24:1-2

Endnotes

All word references and meanings are taken from the James Strong, LLD, STD, The New Strong's Expanded Exhaustive Concordance of the Bible (Red Letter Edition), Nashville, TN: Thomas Nelson Publishers, 2010.

Old Testament word meanings are taken from the Hebrew and Aramaic Dictionary (p. 1 through p. 303) and New Testament word meanings are taken from the Greek Dictionary (p. 1 through p. 277) in the back section of The New Strong's Expanded Exhaustive Concordance of the Bible.

[1] **God Almighty** Hebrew Strong's number 410 / 7706
[2] **Jacob** Hebrew Strong's number 3290
[3] **Jehovah / Lord** Hebrew Strong's number 3068
[4] **Abba** Greek Strong's number 5
[5] **Creature** Greek Strong's number 293
[6] **Covereth** Hebrew Strong's number 5526
[7] **Fire** Hebrew Strong's number 784
[8] **Stones** Hebrew Strong's number 68
[9] **Mountain** Hebrew Strong's number 2022
[10] **Cherub** Hebrew Strong's number 3742

11 **Tabrets** Hebrew Strong's number 8596

12 **Wisdom** Hebrew Strong's number 8454

13 **Understanding** Hebrew Strong's number 998

14 **Possessed** Hebrew Strong's number 7069

15 **Overcometh** Greek Strong's number 3528

16 **Understanding** Greek Strong's number 4907

17 **Mystery** Greek Strong's number 3466

18 **Nod** Hebrew Strong's number 5113

19 **Day** Hebrew Strong's number 3117

20 **Darkness** Hebrew Strong's number 2822

21 **Light** Hebrew Strong's number 216

22 **Life** Greek Strong's number 2222

23 **Light** Greek Strong's number 5457

24 **Darkness** Greek Strong's number 4653

25 **Comprehended** Greek Strong's number 2638

26 **Spirit** Hebrew Strong's number 7307

27 **God** Hebrew Strong's number 430

28 **Image** Hebrew Strong's number 6754

29 **Likeness** Hebrew Strong's number 1823

30 **Tishbite** Hebrew Strong's number 8664

31 **Threshingfloor** Hebrew Strong's number 1637

32 **Experience** Greek Strong's number 1382

Printed in the United States
By Bookmasters